# Jerry Dona...
# Telemaster Guitar

Fender guitars courtesy of Fender Musical Instrument Corporation
Project Manager: Aaron Stang
Editor: Hemme Luttjeboer
Cover Design: Joann Carrera

WARNER BROS. PUBLICATIONS - THE GLOBAL LEADER IN PRINT
USA: 15800 NW 48th Avenue, Miami, FL 33014

WARNER/CHAPPELL MUSIC

NUOVA CARISCH

INTERNATIONAL MUSIC PUBLICATIONS LIMITED

CANADA: 85 SCARSDALE ROAD, SUITE 101
DON MILLS, ONTARIO, M3B 2R2
SCANDINAVIA: P.O. BOX 533, VENDEVAGEN 85 B
S-182 15, DANDERYD, SWEDEN
AUSTRALIA: P.O. BOX 353
3 TALAVERA ROAD, NORTH RYDE N.S.W. 2113

ITALY: VIA M.F. QUINTILIANO 40
20138 MILANO
SPAIN: MAGALLANES, 25
28015 MADRID

ENGLAND: SOUTHEND ROAD,
WOODFORD GREEN, ESSEX IG8 8HN
FRANCE: 25 RUE DE HAUTEVILLE, 75010 PARIS
GERMANY: MARSTALLISTR. 8, D-80539 MUNCHEN
DENMARK: DANMUSIK, VOGNMAGERGADE 7
DK 1120 KOBENHAVNK

# HELLECASTERS

Will Ray  John Jorgenson  Jerry Donahue

# Jerry Donahue's Telemaster Guitar

## Contents

# About The Book

Jerry Donahue reigns over one of the most unique and unmistakably individual guitar styles today. His uncanny technique, melding country, bluegrass, Celtic, folk and rock 'n' roll together into one genre, mirrors his various influences. Not one to rest complacent, he continuously explores and even surpasses his own boundaries and achievements. His recordings with numerous diverse groups such as Fairport Convention, Joan Armatrading and Gerry Rafferty, to name just a few, lay testament to Jerry's skill as an accompanist. His sound and guitar technique are instantly identifiable. After two solo releases he still charts unexplored territory as a member of THE HELLECASTERS with John Jorgenson and Will Ray. This book dispels the mystery of Jerry's style and should inspire you to adopt some of his guitarisms into your own vocabulary.

Jerry Donahue with Signature Stratocaster®

# Introduction

Jerry breaks his style down into categories such as licks and endings based on banjo phrases, steel guitar and "chicken picking." If you are a novice of the guitar, take your time and play back the accompanying CD as often as you need. Jerry demonstrates various examples at different tempos and all the music has been written out with his fingerings. But experiment with your own approaches, too. His trademarks, the "behind the nut" bend and "contrary-motion" bending, both emulate the sounds of a pedal-steel guitar and are techniques that require close scrutiny from even the most accomplished player.

Jerry gives us a workout with two of his original tunes, "The Beak" and "Mixed Emotions." Both are dazzling displays of his talent. As with each music example, these two pieces have been meticulously transcribed in standard notation, including tablature, with correct left-hand fingerings. However, also apply your own fingerings as you incorporate the numerous licks and lines into your vocabulary.

Jerry Donahue Custom Shop Telecaster®

Jerry Donahue Signature Stratocaster®

# Licks And Endings

In this first section Jerry gets right to the heart of his style. His use of sustained open strings is based on banjo type phrases and represents an integral approach in creating shimmering lines. His first few examples may need a little preparation if you are not familiar with this approach to guitar playing. To achieve fluidity with these lines practice them slowly and pay close attention to both right- and left-hand fingerings.

The first prep. example consists of an E minor pentatonic scale using open strings. Your fingers may resemble a "spider's walk" as they descend down the scale. Hold on to each note as long as possible before releasing to sound the next one. The next prep. example is an A minor pentatonic scale followed by a simple C major scale. Tackle only a few notes at a time to get the feel and sound of the patterns. Just remember to let each line "ring out."

## Prep. #1

### E Minor Pentatonic Scale

m = middle finger
p = pick/thumb
a = ring finger

## Prep. #2

### A Minor Pentatonic Scale

## Prep. #3

### C Scale

## ③ *Example 1*

This first example is comprised of notes from the C major scale. Sustain the fretted notes as much as possible. Beat four in the second measure requires a bend from "behind the nut." Practice this a few times at a slow tempo and accelerate only as you become more familiar with both left- and right-hand coordination. These open-string gems yield dazzling results at brisk tempos.

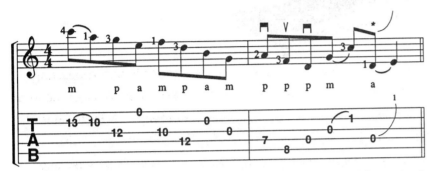

*Behind the Nut Bend.

## ④ *Example 2*

Here is an ending comprised of notes from the G major scale. Again, watch your right and left hand, but note the exceptional stretch in your left hand in order to sustain the line. Experiment with other locations for these notes and use open strings wherever they may occur.

# Behind The Nut Bends

The techniques in this book involve a lot of string bending. Aside from the regular across the fingerboard bends, you will also develop individual string bends from behind the nut. In order to do this properly use light gauge stainless-steel strings (.09-.42, the lighter the better). It is best to use a guitar without a fixed locking nut. The headstock of the guitar must be of the Fender variety—angled headstocks don't allow enough distance between the string and the wood for bending. Telecaster-style headstocks seem to work best for this technique, allowing enough distance to bend a minor, or even a major, 3rd.

## ⑤ Example 3A

Start with a simple bend using open strings and practice going up in 1/2 step increments, like this E minor to E major. Do this gradually until your left-hand fingers are comfortable enough to perform without pain or difficulty.

## ⑥ Example 3B

Here is a whole step bend into A major using two strings. Try the strings one at a time to hear the intended pitch, and then sound them together. Add some vibrato for a nice finish.

## ⑦ *Example 3C*

Equally as challenging is this bend into A minor. The second string moves up a 1/2 step while the third string moves up a whole step. This one can be tricky at first. Exerting the right amount of pressure behind the nut is crucial.

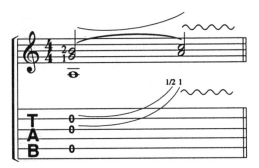

## ⑧ *Example 3D*

Here is a distinctive "behind the nut" bend. It involves contrary motion. This means two notes moving in opposite directions. One note goes upward while another note goes down. In this example, the open 5th string is "pre-bent" a whole step to B. At the same time, the open 4th string is played. Note the left-hand fingerings as you slowly release the pre-bend and bend up on the 4th string. The lick resolves nicely into an A5 chord. It is tricky but very effective.

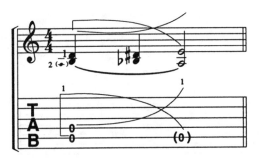

## ⑨ *Example 3E and Example 3F*

You can achieve a whammy bar type sound, or "growl," on the low strings as well. Once your fingers can really handle "behind the nut" bends, try raising the 6th string all the way up 2 and 1/2 steps to A. Do the same for the 5th string and bend it up 2 and 1/2 steps to D. Add a touch of vibrato at the end of each bend.

Example 3E

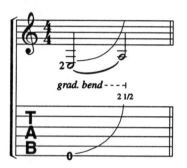

Example 3F

## ⑩ *Example 4: Lick from "Around the Bend"*

This is an example in E major with a third string 1/2 step pre-bend to G♯. This note is then extended another 1 and 1/2 steps to B. These movements are credited to the left-hand index finger behind the nut and all takes place on the first beat! The other important bend in this phrase comes at the end. Again, add vibrato as you hold the final note.

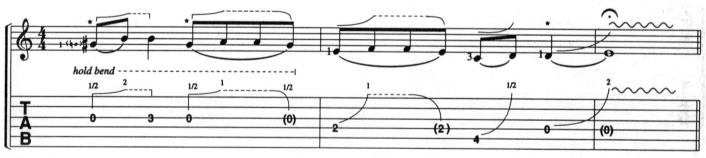

*B.N.B.

## ⑪ *Example 5A*

Here we have a double bend that developed virtually by accident. Catch the 2nd string while releasing the 3rd string bend and raise it up a 1/2 step. This creates a rather nice pedal-steel guitar effect. The whole action is played with the left-hand index finger!

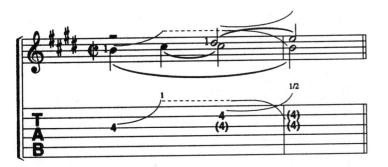

## ⑫ *Example 5B*

Same idea with a little embellishment.

⑬ # Example 5C

This phrase is more involved but yields the same pedal-steel guitar effect. Watch the pre-bend on beat three. Your intonation must be accurate for these to be convincing. The line concludes with the double bend. Try using a volume pedal and sprinkle a little swell onto each bend. This kind of note manipulation can be very effective.

⑭ # Example 6

Let's take the double bend a little further this time and finish it by emphasizing the dominant sound of the A9 chord. Just watch the fingerings and let the notes ring.

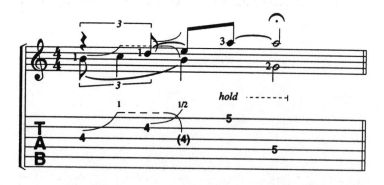

15 # *Example 7*

Here is a double bend in E major with a fourth string bend to fatten up the sound. This one may be tough at first until you coordinate your fingers properly. The steel-string ending starts with a fourth string bend on the first beat that is held as you play a double string bend on the second and third strings. The bends on the fourth and third strings are released on beat one of measure two at the same time as the second string bends up a half step. Make sure you can hear all the bend resolutions that form the E triad.

16 # *Example 8A: Parallel Motion Double Bend*

This time we'll bend two strings in the same direction. This lick is a simple V-I resolution in D major. As you bend the third string up a whole step, bend the second string along with it—but, it remains silent until beat three. The first note is sustained as the second string sounds and both bends are released to a D major double-stop in the second measure.

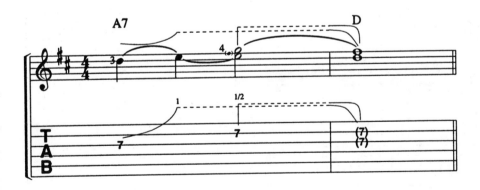

**⑰ *Example 8B***

This is a more musical approach to basically the same phrase as in the previous example. Adding the first string to the line treats us to a beautiful steel-guitar shimmer. Notice how each bend resolves independently of each other and how all the notes are held right into the second measure.

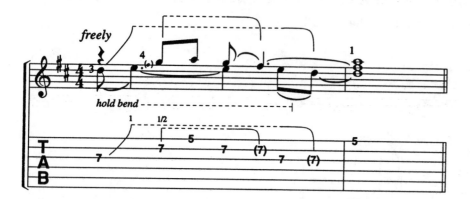

**⑱ *Example 9***

Here we hint at a bit of "chicken picking" in this phrase. It involves a third string bend, in A7, that is held in tandem with notes that descend chromatically and resolve to D major. Slowly release the F♯ bend onto the second beat as you pick the notes on the second string with your right-hand middle finger. (More on "chicken picking" later.)

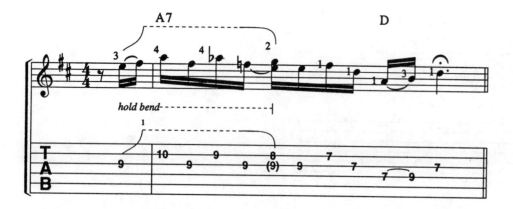

## [19] *Example 10*

This example starts on the V7 (E7) chord and resolves to I (A). This pattern makes its way to the A chord with a series of double-stops and a slow release bend on the third string. It is essential that you follow the correct fingerings for this one. You can invent your own once you are comfortable playing the line at a snappy tempo. Slowly release the third string bend while you play the stops on the first and second strings.

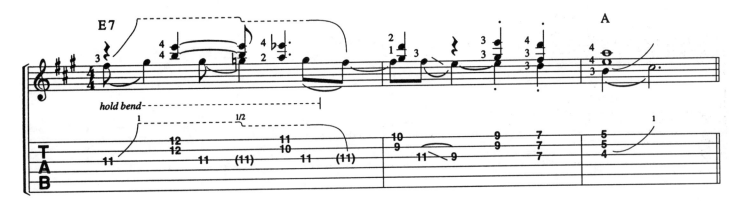

## [20] *Example 11*

Here is a typical steel-guitar lick. It requires a stretch with the left hand. Before playing the A on the first string, pre-bend the F# bend on the third string. Sustain all the notes in the first measure before resolving to the E double-stop bend in the second measure. Explore variations of this one on your own.

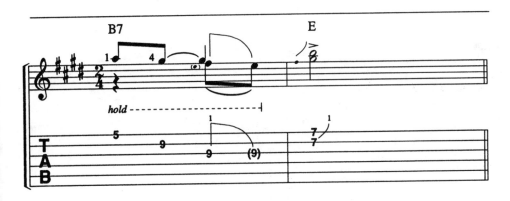

## 21 Example 12: Banjo-Style Intro or Ending

This two measure lick can be used as an intro or an ending. It is written in the key of G major and the bluegrass-tinged flavor of the line nudges at the blues with the B♭ note throughout. The open second, third and fourth strings conveniently denote a G major triad. Watch your left- and right-hand fingerings and practice the line slowly. The phrase is most effective at a quick tempo.

## 22 Example 13: Diminished Run

The key to effectively mastering this tricky line is to hold on to, and sustain, each group of 16th notes after the initial hammer or slide. With correct left- and right-hand coordination you should succeed in playing it at the same tempo as the recording. The first measure outlines a D diminished scale and segues into an A7 to D major resolution. It's a great lick to end a tune.

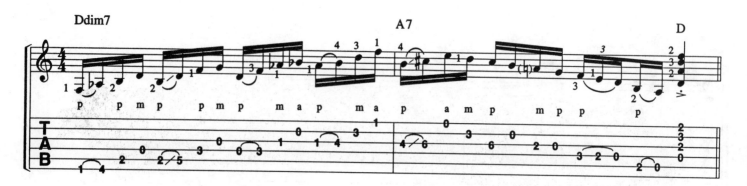

## 23 *Example 14*

Here is basically the same idea but in a different key. It starts with a C# diminished line and is followed by a barrage of triplets over D7 to G major. The same dynamics apply to the diminished scale as in the previous example. Quite effective at a brisk tempo.

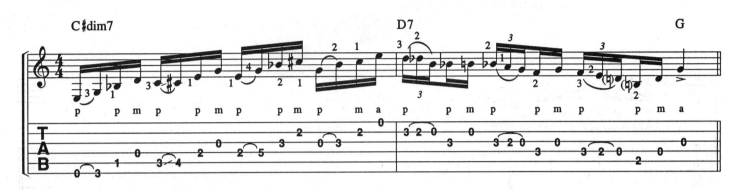

# Right-Hand Picking Techniques

**(24)**

Jerry's technique includes his deft use of both right-hand fingers and a pick. In his formative years as a guitar student he played a classical guitar as a prerequisite to acquiring an electric guitar. Only after displaying a serious attitude toward the instrument did he progress on to the electric. He was eager to play rock 'n' roll, and the combination of pick and fingers developed into his country and banjo techniques. Today he uses this style for almost all of his playing. Along with the pick, Jerry elicits notes with his right-hand middle and ring finger, and sometimes even the pinkie as well.

**(25)** ## Example 15

To get you started, try this one with your pick, middle and ring fingers. Practice slowly to develop coordination. You should aim for a clean, smooth roll like a banjo player.

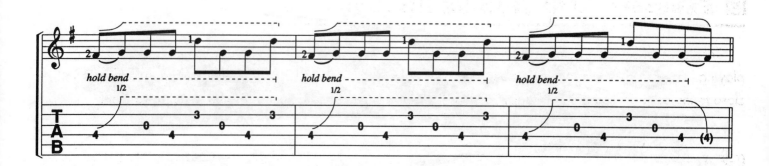

## 26 *Example 16*

This is a variation of the previous line that uses slides, bends and even "behind the nut" bends for special effects. Practice slowly and work up the tempo each time.

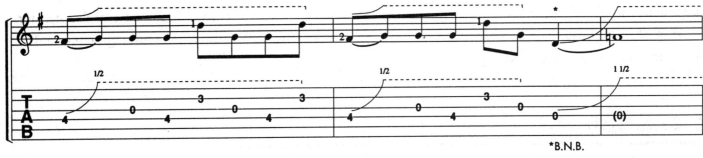

*B.N.B.

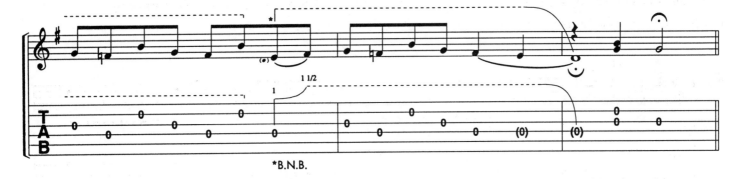

*B.N.B.

## 27 *Example 17A: Chicken Picking*

The sound of staccato notes imitating a chicken is probably the easiest way to describe this style of guitar playing. You can play this style a number of ways. In this line use your pick with the thumb and index finger very close to the edge so you get a "snappy" sound. Right-hand strokes have been indicated to help you along.

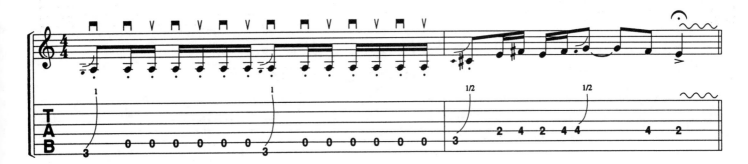

## [28] *Example 17B*

To achieve this crisp and clean sound, use your pick and alternate with your middle finger. This method should provide the quick succession of 16th notes with the "chicken picking" sound. Like all the techniques in this book, it takes a great amount of patience and persistence to master correctly.

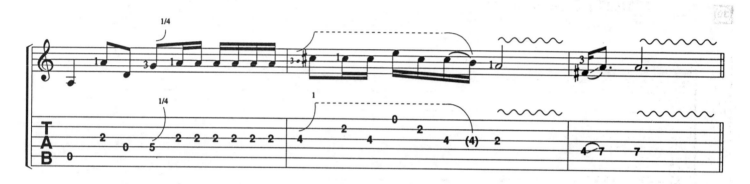

## [29] *Example 17C*

Chicken picking is highly effective in association with double-stops. Semi-mute the notes played with the pick to get a percussive sound. Listen closely and imitate the attack.

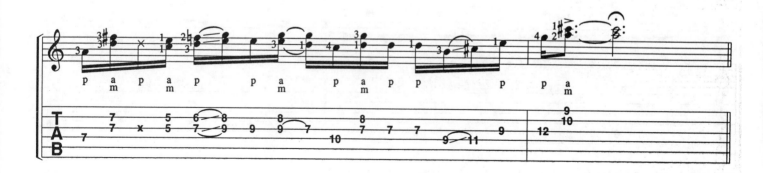

# The Beak

This tune from TELECASTING is chock full of the techniques we have covered including string bends, double-stops and, of course, "behind the nut" bends. Though Jerry effortlessly meanders through the tune in one take, stay tuned as he plays and examines each phrase measure by measure. Take each line slowly and follow the fingerings carefully. However, experiment with your own approach to the lines as well.

**Moderate country** ♩ = 114

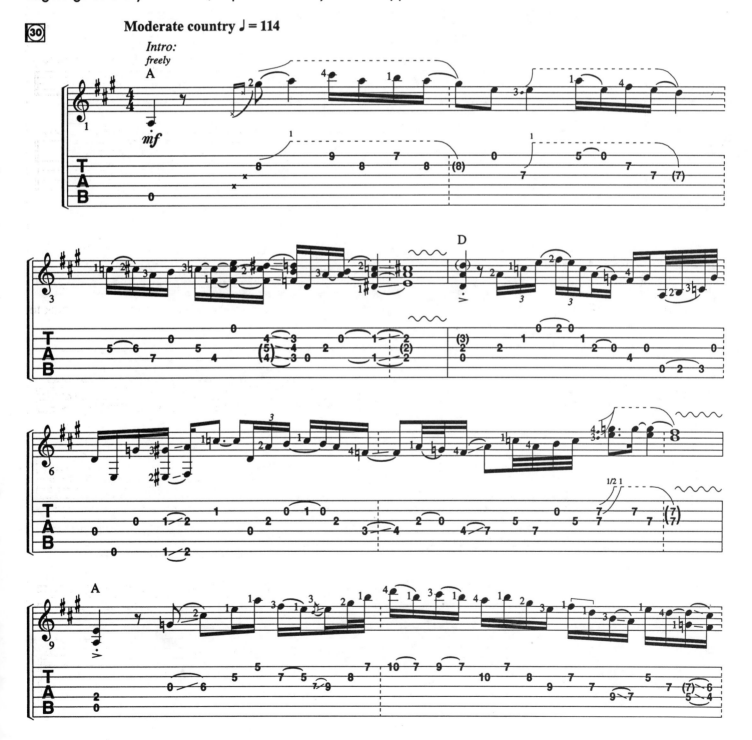

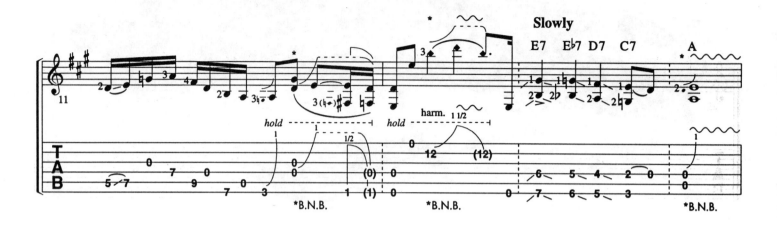

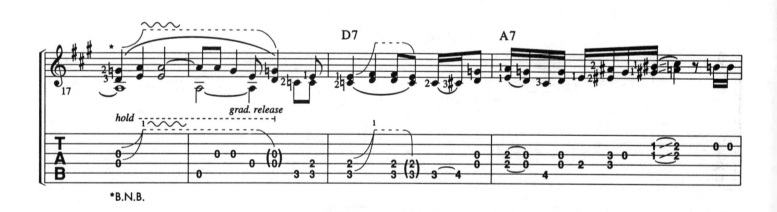

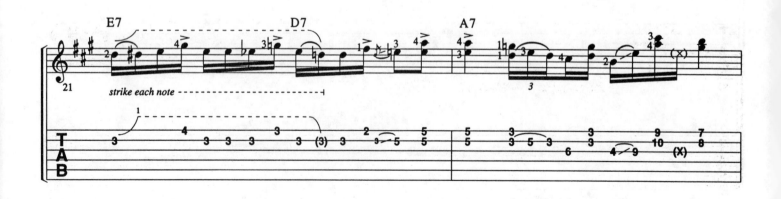

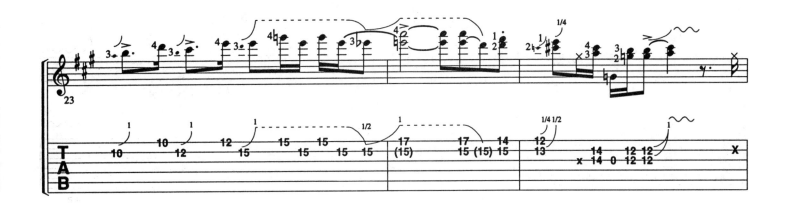

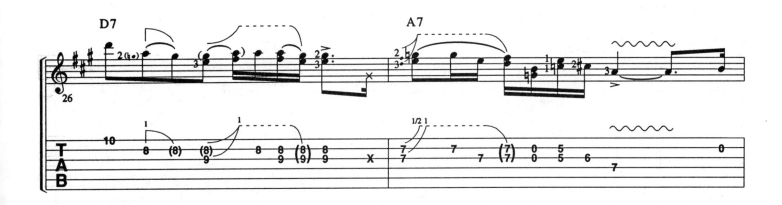

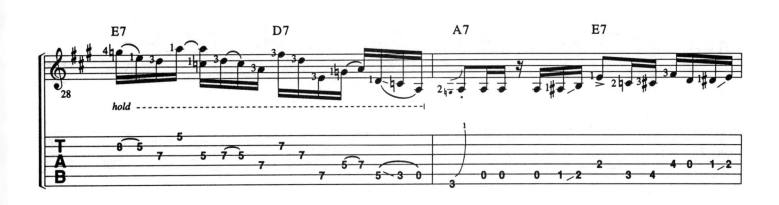

# The Beak Intro

**31**

Phrase One

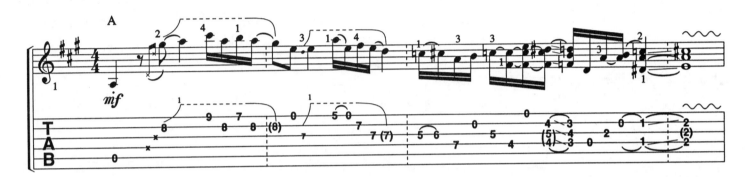

**32**

Phrase Two

**Phrase Three**

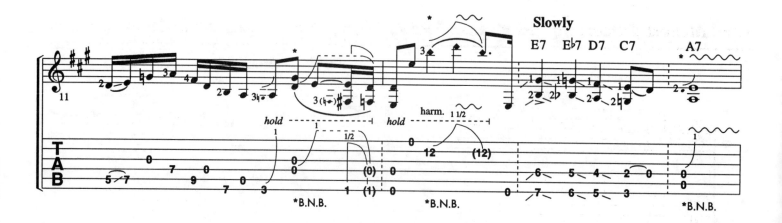

Refer back to the tune transcription, begin at measure 15 marked "a tempo" and follow Jerry in the accompanying CD.

# Mixed Emotions

This dazzling showcase of chicken picking, double-stops, banjo runs and, of course, "behind the nut" bends displays most of the subjects that we have covered in this book. With patience and study you should be able to play along with the recording and soon be creating your own lines. Enjoy!

**35** : "Mixed Emotions" at tempo,  **36** : "Mixed Emotions" at half speed

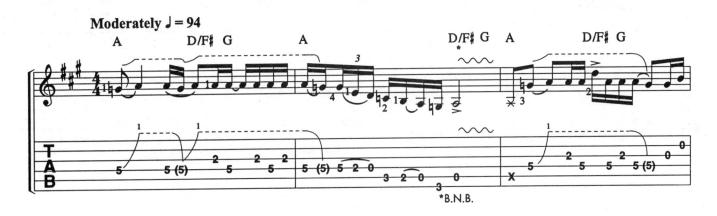

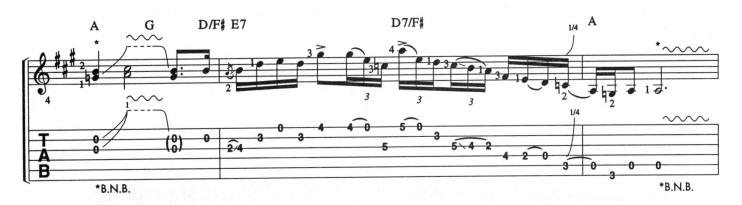

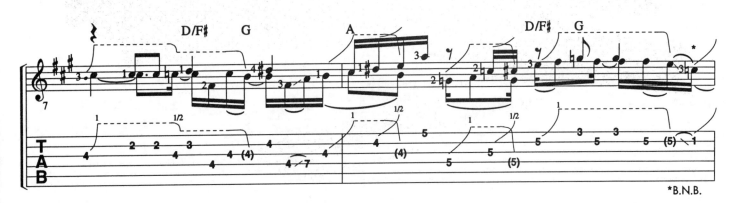

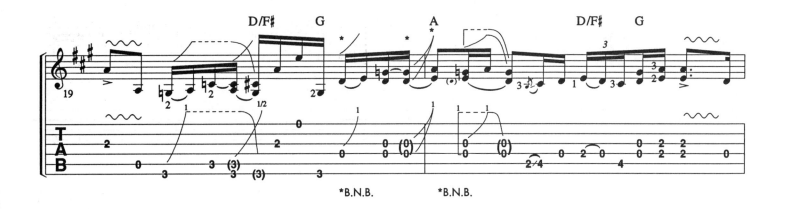

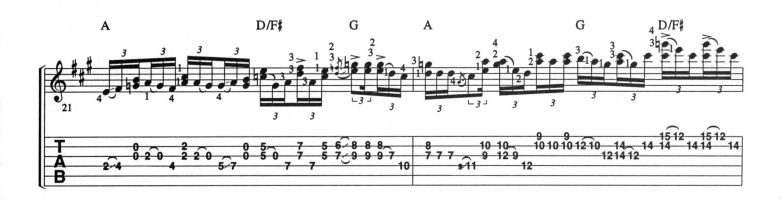

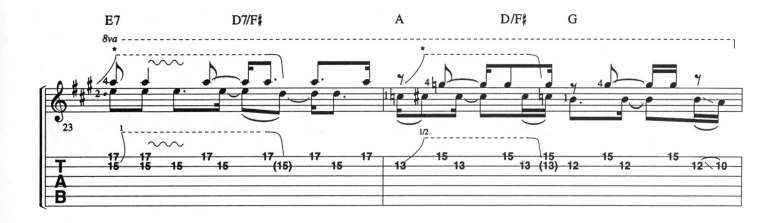

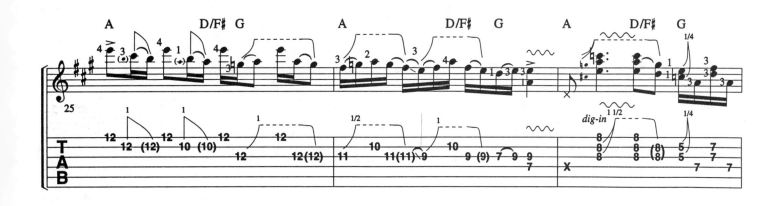

# GUITAR TAB GLOSSARY **

## TABLATURE EXPLANATION

**READING TABLATURE:** Tablature illustrates the six strings of the guitar. Notes and chords are indicated by the placement of fret numbers on a given string(s).

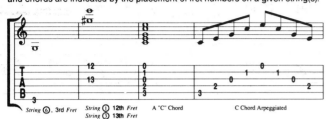

String ⑥, 3rd Fret    String ① 12th Fret    A "C" Chord    C Chord Arpeggiated
String ③ 13th Fret

## BENDING NOTES

**HALF STEP:** Play the note and bend string one half step.*

**WHOLE STEP:** Play the note and bend string one whole step.

**WHOLE STEP AND A HALF:** Play the note and bend string a whole step and a half.

**SLIGHT BEND (Microtone):** Play the note and bend string slightly to the equivalent of half a fret.

**PREBEND (Ghost Bend):** Bend to the specified note, before the string is picked.

**PREBEND AND RELEASE:** Bend the string, play it, then release to the original note.

**REVERSE BEND:** Play the already-bent string, then immediately drop it down to the fretted note.

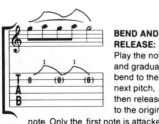

**BEND AND RELEASE:** Play the note and gradually bend to the next pitch, then release to the original note. Only the first note is attacked.

*A half step is the smallest interval in Western music; it is equal to one fret. A whole step equals two frets.

**UNISON BEND:** Play both notes and immediately bend the lower note to the same pitch as the higher note.

**DOUBLE NOTE BEND:** Play both notes and immediately bend both strings simultaneously.

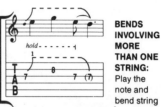

**BENDS INVOLVING MORE THAN ONE STRING:** Play the note and bend string while playing an additional note (or notes) on another string(s). Upon release, relieve pressure from additional note(s), causing original note to sound alone.

**BENDS INVOLVING STATIONARY NOTES:** Play notes and bend lower pitch, then hold until release begins (indicated at the point where line becomes solid).

## TREMOLO BAR

**SPECIFIED INTERVAL:** The pitch of a note or chord is lowered to a specified interval and then may or may not return to the original pitch. The activity of the tremolo bar is graphically represented by peaks and valleys.

**UN-SPECIFIED INTERVAL:** The pitch of a note or a chord is lowered to an unspecified interval.

## HARMONICS

**NATURAL HARMONIC:** A finger of the fret hand lightly touches the note or notes indicated in the tab and is played by the pick hand.

**ARTIFICIAL HARMONIC:** The first tab number is fretted, then the pick hand produces the harmonic by using a finger to lightly touch the same string at the second tab number (in parenthesis) and is then picked by another finger.

**ARTIFICIAL "PINCH" HAR-MONIC:** A note is fretted as indicated by the tab, then the pick hand produces the harmonic by squeezing the pick firmly while using the tip of the index finger in the pick attack. If parenthesis are found around the fretted note, it does not sound. No parenthesis means both the fretted note and A.H. are heard simultaneously.

**By Kenn Chipkin and Aaron Stang

# RHYTHM SLASHES

**STRUM INDICA-TIONS:** Strum with indicated rhythm.

The chord voicings are found on the first page of the transcription underneath the song title.

**INDICATING SINGLE NOTES USING RHYTHM SLASHES:** Very often single notes are incorporated into a rhythm part. The note name is indicated above the rhythm slash with a fret number and a string indication.

# ARTICULATIONS

**HAMMER ON:** Play lower note, then "hammer on" to higher note with another finger. Only the first note is attacked.

**LEFT HAND HAMMER:** Hammer on the first note played on each string with the left hand.

**PULL OFF:** Play higher note, then "pull off" to lower note with another finger. Only the first note is attacked.

**FRET-BOARD TAPPING:** "Tap" onto the note indicated by + with a finger of the pick hand, then pull off to the following note held by the fret hand.

**TAP SLIDE:** Same as fretboard tapping, but the tapped note is slid randomly up the fretboard, then pulled off to the following note.

**BEND AND TAP TECHNIQUE:** Play note and bend to specified interval. While holding bend, tap onto note indicated.

**LEGATO SLIDE:** Play note and slide to the following note. (Only first note is attacked).

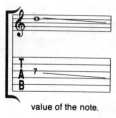

**LONG GLISSAN-DO:** Play note and slide in specified direction for the full value of the note.

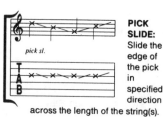

**SHORT GLISSAN-DO:** Play note for its full value and slide in specified direction at the last possible moment.

**PICK SLIDE:** Slide the edge of the pick in specified direction across the length of the string(s).

**MUTED STRINGS:** A percussive sound is made by laying the fret hand across all six strings while pick hand strikes specified area (low, mid, high strings).

**PALM MUTE:** The note or notes are muted by the palm of the pick hand by lightly touching the string(s) near the bridge.

**TREMOLO PICKING:** The note or notes are picked as fast as possible.

**TRILL:** Hammer on and pull off consecutively and as fast as possible between the original note and the grace note.

**ACCENT:** Notes or chords are to be played with added emphasis.

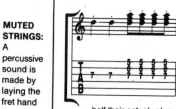

**STACCATO (Detached Notes):** Notes or chords are to be played roughly half their actual value and with separation.

**DOWN STROKES AND UPSTROKES:** Notes or chords are to be played with either a downstroke ( ⊓ ) or upstroke ( ∨ ) of the pick.

**VIBRATO:** The pitch of a note is varied by a rapid shaking of the fret hand finger, wrist, and forearm.